Gerenuk

Fischer's lovebird

East african oryx

Southern ground hornbill

Warthog

African elephant

Lilac-breasted roller

Secretary bird

Marabou stork

Nile crocodile

Superb starling

Red-billed hornbill

Blue wildebeest

Impala

Giant kingfisher

Plains zebra

Kori bustard

Saddle-billed stork

Olive baboon

African spoonbill

Hoopoe

For my parents

Published in the US by Nobrow (US) Inc.
Printed in Belgium on FSC assured paper.

ISBN: 978-1-909263-56-7

Order from www.flyingeyebooks.com

Ella Bailey

ONE DAY
›››› ON OUR ‹‹‹‹
BLUE PLANET

...IN THE SAVANNAH

Flying Eye Books
London – New York

As the morning sun rises on the
African Savannah, a lioness and her cub emerge slowly
from their secret den.

Since this cub's birth, his mother has kept him safe and hidden.
Now he is big, and ready to join the rest of his family, who all live
together in a group called a pride.

These are his aunts,

and here are his cousins.

This is the father of all the cubs.
He is very, very big,

and his roar is very, very loud.

The lions share their home with many other strange and wonderful creatures. The little cub chases his mother's tail through the tall grass...

...to the river for a cool drink, as midday is when the fiery sun burns hottest. Water is very precious on the savannah, sometimes it may not rain for months and months.

Adult lions are very good at relaxing,
and can spend most of their day sleeping,

but this little cub is best at playing!

He loves nothing more than hunting
and growling and stalking and chasing.

The sun begins to set and the air grows cooler.
The lionesses leave the cubs in a safe place…

...now it is time to hunt!

They work together to get closer
... and closer... and closer...

. . . to their prey.

While some animals eat plants, and others eat insects,
a lion's favourite food is meat.

This little lion cub is still very small and
so for now he only needs his mother's milk.

Lions often stay awake during the night,

but this cub has had a very long day...

...so he sleeps under the cool light of the moon...

...until the sun rises once again, on another day on our blue planet.

ANIMALS OF THE AFRICAN SAVANNAH
NIGHTTIME

White-tailed
mongoose

Hooded
vulture

Striped
hyena

Caracal

African savanna hare

Leopard

Aardvark

Ground pangolin

Aardwolf

Black-backed jackal

Bat-eared fox

Springhare